For Fergus — M.M.
For Rosie and her friends in Miss Bailey's class — A.W.

First published in Great Britain in 1999 by Macdonald Young Books,

Macdonald Young Books
an imprint of Wayland Publishers Ltd
61 Western Road
Hove
East Sussex
BN3 1JD

You can find Macdonald Young Books on the internet at:
http://www.myb.co.uk

Commissioning Editor Dereen Taylor
Editor Rosie Nixon
Designer Liz Black
Science and Language Consultant Dr Carol Ballard

Moss, Miriam
    Take a walk on a rainbow: a first look at colour.
    (MYBees)
    1. Colours - Juvenile Literature
    I. Title
    535.6

Printed and bound in Asa, Portugal

ISBN   07500 2778 9

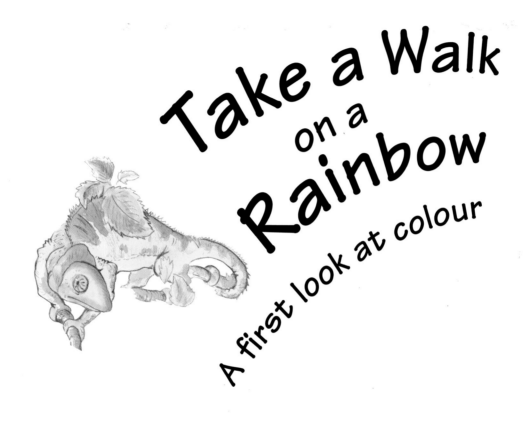

Take a Walk on a Rainbow

on a

Rainbow

A first look at colour

Take a Walk
on a
Rainbow
A first look at colour

by Miriam Moss

MacDonald Young Books

Storm clouds gather and the sky turns black.

6

When there's no light there's no colour.

CRACK! Lightning flashes

8

and Tilly's room lights up with colour.

made up of all the colours of the rainbow.

The sun shines through raindrops in the air

Let's take a walk on the rainbow!

making sunlight spread out into all the colours of the rainbow.

14

if it's safe to cross the road.

Some fruit changes

Can I have a banana please?

colour when it's ripe.

Make sure you pick a nice ripe yellow one.

Birds can see many colours. Cats, dogs and

Do you think that birds and animals see colours like we do?

Well that bird can see those red berries!

horses only see in black, white and grey.

20

"Look at that red frog Grandad!"

The bright red colour of the

22

poisonous frog warns the monkey not to touch it.

26

Yellow and blue makes green.

Mix up all the colours and new ones can be seen!

What's at the end of our rainbow Tilly?

Home of course!

Every night the sun goes down, light

fades and everything looks black and grey again.

29

Mix it up!

The light that shines from the sun looks white, but it's really made up of all the colours of the rainbow.

See for yourself when you spin this simple colour wheel. All the colours will mix together and look white before your eyes!

To make the wheel:

1 Cut out a circle of card

2 Colour it like this:

3 Stick a pencil through the middle.

4 Spin it!

Useful words

Chameleon
A small lizard living in hot countries. A chameleon can hide by changing its skin to the same colour as the things around it.

Lightning
Giant flashes of light that break out of thunder clouds during a storm. You can see the lightning flash before you hear the sound of thunder.

Rainbow
An arch in the sky made of lots of colours. A rainbow appears when white light from the sun shines through raindrops in the air. The raindrops make the white light spread out into all the colours of the rainbow.

Storm
Bad weather. There can be strong winds, rain or snow and sometimes thunder and lightning.

OTHER M.Y.Bees FOR YOU TO ENJOY:

Paint a Sun in the Sky – a first look
at the seasons
Claire Llewellyn
Illustrated by Amanda Wood
ISBN: 07500 2787 8

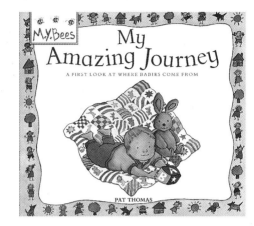

My Amazing Journey – a first look
at where babies come from
Pat Thomas
Illustrated by Lesley Harker
ISBN: 07500 2573 5

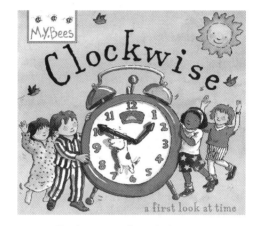

Clockwise – a first look at time
Sam Godwin
Illustrated by Anthony Lewis

ISBN: 07500 2664 2

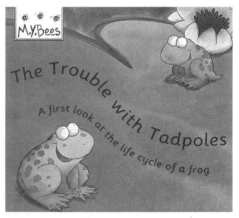

The Trouble with Tadpoles – a
first look at the life cycle of a frog
Sam Godwin
Illustrated by Simone Abel
ISBN: 07500 2652 9

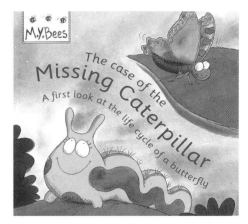

The Case of the Missing Caterpillar – a first look
at the life cycle of a butterfly
Sam Godwin
Illustrated by Simone Abel
ISBN: 07500 2651 0

A Seed in Need – a first look
at the plant cycle
Sam Godwin
Illustrated by Simone Abel
ISBN: 07500 2496 8

All these books and many more can be purchased from your local bookseller. For more information, write to:

The Sales Department   Macdonald Young Books   61 Western Road   Hove   BN3 1JD